DEAR MR. PRESIDENT,

REAGAN KENNEDY'S LETTER

by

Lisa McDougall

To Alyce, Herb, Cindy, Caitlyn and Chuck-
for teaching me about the nature of life and the life of nature.

ISBN-13: 978-1545214046
Library of Congress Control Number: 2017908563
CreateSpace Independent Publishing Platform

Layout and design by Janna Willoughby-Lohr of Papercraft Miracles
www.papercraftmiracles.com

8% of the net profits from this book will be divided evenly and donated to the following
not-for-profit organizations that help protect our environment:
The Nature Conservancy, The Everglades Foundation, Greenpeace,
and The National Audubon Society.

Dear Everybody,

Thank you for looking at my book. I hope you decide to read it and that it makes you think. When I grow up, I want to be a scientist. In science independent thinking is especially important because science is really about finding the truth. When I wrote my letter to President Trump I didn't use any footnotes or pictures, but then I made the letter into this book. Footnotes give more information about a subject and help you research things for yourself, important for independent thinking, so I decided to put some in the book. Each footnote is marked with a foot (like this: 👣) and then at the bottom of the page there is more information you can use to check out what I am saying, or to dig deeper. I think the pictures just make it more fun.

I hear so much about "fake" news and "fake" science, I want you to judge for yourself. After you investigate and think about it, I think you will agree there is strong science to back me up on my worries over our planet's health. The resources in the footnotes can lead you to some pretty cool stuff, get you started on finding things you and your family can do to help our planet, build on what you already know and maybe give you some ideas for writing your own letter to President Trump.

You might also find some ideas you disagree with. In a couple of the footnotes I have included stuff I disagree with, like some climate change deniers' ideas because it is good to know what people who disagree with you think, so you can reach an informed conclusion and maybe even persuade them to see your point. I read what the climate change deniers had to say and I believe they are wrong. So do most scientists.

I think I will write the President every so often to let him know how he is doing. Maybe you want to write him too. If a lot of kids write President Trump, he would know what we think and he might be more likely to make choices that benefit our country and our planet. If enough of us write we'll have our own movement and that would sure get his attention. We can let him know we are paying attention and thank him for any good things he does and tell him if he goes wrong. Let's hope he is a good steward of our planet and resources, but let's be ready to take positive steps if he is not.

Here's where to write him:

> President Donald J. Trump
> The White House
> 1600 Pennsylvania Avenue NW
> Washington, DC 20500

I hope he cares what kids think because even though we can't vote we are the future. Plus, our parents can vote and they care about us and their grandchildren to come. Stay green!

R.K.

PREFACE
(Aimed at parents but kids can read it too)

Is there any basis for hope that the future health of our children, our country and our planet during and following the Trump presidency will be at least a cut above critical? Are these the last days for animals such as gorillas, Bengal tigers and giraffes in the wild? Will polar bears become extinct? Will our kids be able to swim and drink water that doesn't expose them to toxins? Breathe clean air? Can Reagan Kennedy, other children and voiceless animals get Trump to be his best self and leave a legacy of hope? Is Reagan reflecting our collective thoughts - hope for the best but prepare for the worst? What does that preparation look like? What steps can and should each of us take to keep our planet from circling the drain?

We are all watching. Turn the pages in the book as the pages of history are turned by the 45th president of the United States, Donald J. Trump.

MY LETTER TO PRESIDENT TRUMP

April 6, 2017
President Donald J. Trump
The White House
1600 Pennsylvania Avenue NW
Washington, DC 20500

Dear President Trump,

   I see you on TV a lot. You lived in a ginormous Tower in New York City until you moved into the White House in Washington D.C., after you became President.

1

GINORMOUS

TRUMP TOWER OF POWER

You and your family lived on the top floors in a penthouse where your front door is covered with gold and diamonds (well, at least that's what some photos show). Does the Tower really have its' own waterfall?? The views from your penthouse must be amazing. I don't know too much about New York City geography but I bet you can see Central Park, all over the city and even the Statue of Liberty! You are so high up that all the people on the ground must look like insignificant little specks of dirt.

I read that when people come to visit you in your beautiful home they are supposed to take off their shoes. Actually, we do that at our house too because otherwise our house (not as fancy as yours, but nice for us) gets all tracked up with mud and snow and other things from outside. I guess removing your shoes is common in a lot of cultures because my friends from Taiwan also remove their shoes and so do lots of other people who come visit.

I heard you are very rich, famous and powerful and lots of other people who are mostly also rich, famous and powerful come to talk with you. You meet with them and listen to their ideas so that you can be a good president.

On TV I see the four gold elevators in the fancy marble lobby of your Tower of Power going up and down with lots of very important people.

8 a.m.

Noon

3 p.m.

5 p.m.

1600 Pennsylvania Avenue NW
Washington DC
20500

HOME SWEET HOME

By the time you get to read this, you will probably be settled in and call the White House your new home.

You say you are really, really smart, which is very important for ruling our country, America. I also heard you got excellent marks, did very, very well at a great school, hard to get into, the Wharton School (not the Hogwarts School of Witchcraft and Wizardry, which is also a great school and hard to get into, LOL!).

WHARTON SCHOOL
REPORT CARD
(IMAGINED)

Donald J. Trump - Student

Reading	A+
Writing	A+
Math	A+
Science	C -
Music	A+
Art	A+
Gym	A+

It has been a pleasure getting to know Donald this semester. He tackles assignments with great gusto! In any group discussion, he is the most active participant. Choosing Debate Club as an extracurricular, was a really smart move. Donald (or "the Donald" a moniker he has chosen) loves to share his ideas and communicates with flair, although sometimes at the cost of precision. Next semester his goal should be to lessen the hyperbole and sharpen his oral communication skills, aiming for greater clarity , so there is no ambiguity in his message. He perseveres like no other student I have ever seen. Donald loves to impress. Expect great things from your son!

At my school some kids have said they think you will be a bad President because you are not interested in science and don't care about the environment. They say that when they grow up pollution and global warming will have killed off a lot of life and there won't be clean water or air and all the wild animals will be gone or in a zoo. Very sad.

But I said you are really, really smart, so of course you are interested in science and you love your family, children and grandchildren and have a good heart, so of course you care.

My brother showed me a copy of a letter from back in 2009 that you sent to President Obama and the United States Congress telling them the government should strengthen laws that fight global warming and mentioning that science shows it will be awful bad for us and our planet if things aren't taken care of quick. You pointed out how it would not only help the planet but also be good for the economy. Your children signed the letter too. Smart kids! I figure you must believe very strongly in a clean and healthy planet and also believe that letters to our leaders can be very important, for you to send off a letter like that. You helped give me the idea to write you (although I won't be able to print mine in the New York Times! LOL!). Yours was a good letter, Mr. President!

I am thinking the kids who say you will be bad are wrong and, in fact, you will be good for our country and our planet where we all live.

A copy of the letter I'm referring to can be found on the next page of this book or by following this link: http://grist.org/politics/donald-trump-climate-action-new-york-times/

Dear President Obama
& The United States Congress,

Tomorrow
leaders from 192 countries
will gather at

The UN Climate Change Conference
in Copenhagen

to determine
the fate of our planet.

As business leaders we are optimistic that President Obama is attending Copenhagen with emissions targets. Additionally, we urge you, our government, to strengthen and pass United States legislation, and lead the world by example. We support your effort to ensure meaningful and effective measures to control climate change, an immediate challenge facing the United States and the world today. Please don't postpone the earth. If we fail to act now, it is scientifically irrefutable that there will be catastrophic and irreversible consequences for humanity and our planet.

We recognize the key role that American innovation and leadership play in stimulating the worldwide economy. Investing in a Clean Energy Economy will drive state-of-the-art technologies that will spur economic growth, create new energy jobs, and increase our energy security all while reducing the harmful emissions that are putting our planet at risk. We have the ability and the know-how to lead the world in clean energy technology to thrive in a global market and economy. But we must embrace the challenge today to ensure that future generations are left with a safe planet and a strong economy.

Please allow us, the United States of America, to serve in modeling the change necessary to protect humanity and our planet.

In partnership,

Chris Anderson, Curator, TED Richard Baker, Chairman, Lord & Taylor Dan, David & Laureen Barber, Blue Hill Chris Blackwell, Founder, Island Records, Island Outpost Graydon Carter, Editor, Vanity Fair Deepak Chopra, Adjunct Professor, Kellogg School of Business and Management Yvon Chouinard, Founder, Patagonia Ben Cohen, Jerry Greenfield, Co-founders, Ben & Jerry's Gregory Colbert, Creator, Ashes & Snow Kenneth Cole, Chairman, Kenneth Cole Paulette Cole, CEO & Creative Director, ABC Home, ABC Carpet & Home Tom Colicchio, Chef & Owner, Craft Restaurants Kit Crawford, Gary Erickson, Co-Owners & Co-CEOs, Clif Bar & Company Steve Ells, Founder, Chairman & Co-CEO, Chipotle Mexican Grill, Inc. Eileen Fisher, CEO, Eileen Fisher Walt Freese, CEO, Ben & Jerry's Homemade Mitchell Gold, Chairman, Bob Williams, President, Co-Founders, Mitchell Gold + Bob Williams Matt Goldman, Co-Founder & CEO, Blue Man Group Seth Goldman, CEO, Honest Tea Robert Grebler, Founder, Pokonobe Associates, Jenga Licensor Adrian Grenier, Reckless Productions Alan Hassenfeld, former Chairman, Hasbro, Inc. Don Hazen, Executive Editor, AlterNet Gary Hirshberg, CEO, Stonyfield Yogurt Jeffrey Hollender, CEO, Seventh Generation Kate Hudson, David Babaii, Co-Founders, David Babaii for WildAid Mike Kaplan, CEO, Aspen Skiing Company Michael Kieschnick, President, Credo Mobile Sheryl Leach, Creator & Founder of Barney Sven-Olof Lindblad, Founder, Lindblad Expeditions Danny Meyer, CEO, Union Square Hospitality Group Laura Michalchyshyn, President and GM, Planet Green, Discovery Communications Will Raap, Chairman & Founder, Gardener's Supply Company Horst Rechelbacher, Founder, Aveda, Founder & CEO, Intelligent Nutrients David Rockwell, Founder & Owner, Rockwell Group Maury Rubin, Founder, Chef & CEO, City Bakery, Birdbath Green Bakery Michael Rupp, CEO & President, The Rockport Company Gordon Segal, Chairman, Crate & Barrel Jeff Skoll, Founder, Participant Media and Skoll Foundation Harvey Spevak, CEO, Equinox Greg Steltenpohl, Founder, Odwalla Michelle Stein, President, Aeffe USA Martha Stewart, Founder, Martha Stewart Living Omnimedia, Inc. Jeffrey Swartz, CEO, Timberland Tom Szaky, CEO, TerraCycle Donald J. Trump, Chairman and President, Donald J. Trump Jr., EVP, Eric F. Trump, EVP, Ivanka M. Trump, EVP, The Trump Organization Jean-Georges Vongerichten, Executive Chef & Owner, Jean-Georges Management LLC

That's you and your kids, right?

if you want to go quickly, go alone. if you want to go far, go together. african proverb

Business leaders, sign onto this initiative: businessleaders4environmentalchange.us

9

I bet you get back to your Trump Tower of Power sometimes and I wish the fancy gold elevator could carry some of my favorite things, the animals and little creatures, up to talk with you so they could help you be a good President. The important people are telling you about their ideas and worries, so the animals should too, except since they can't talk I am writing you this letter to make sure you know about our animal friends and all the small creatures, which are really important for what is called the balance of nature.

You know what I wish for? A planet that is healthy for all living things. There is a good story my Mother used to read me about how all the animals could talk on Christmas Eve. I can't say that I have heard them talk, but I am pretty sure they would say they want a healthy planet where they can live in peace in the wild places they call home.

Sometimes changes to the environment result in consequences that we cannot see for a long time. I am just a kid, but I will have to try to make the best of what happens to our planet under your watch and so will other kids. You are the steward of our future. Please think of us and the other creatures.

Photo by John Rocany, Daily News Archive via Getty Images

Mar-A-Lago

Even if you don't get back to Trump Tower, there is your "Winter Whitehouse", "Mar-A-Lago", where you could host the animals. (If you don't want them visiting the White House, that is!) Awesome oceanfront palace! They say it has marble everything except for the stuff that is gold and crystal. On the exterior there are statues of a parrot, a monkey, a ram, an eagle and a griffin. It looks so cool. You have the best places to go, summer, winter and in-between.

Everglades Foundation

I just knew you were interested in the environment and did some research about that. When I read about how you supported Everglades restoration by hosting a fund raiser in 2006 at Mar-A-Lago for the Everglades Foundation 👣 I was even more sure. Plus, it shows you have wild animal hosting experience, because I heard an alligator, an owl and a panther all made the guest list for that glitzy gala. You don't want Mar-A-Lago to be one of those exclusive clubs where nobody can get in, right? Good job!

👣 At evergladesfoundation.org you can find out all about what they do. They have internships and scholarships. Read about the Barley Prize, where they are trying to solve a "wicked waste water" problem — phosphorous water pollution. Is there a prize? Oh yes, Ten Million Dollars!

Dinner at Mar-a-Lago

The Everglades Foundation is important because the Everglades is on life-support. The Foundation's goal is restore the Everglades to its natural state. One part of the Foundation's strategy is to promote Everglades literacy- make sure people know its importance as a resource, and which actions help and which hurt.

Another part is using the knowledge and research findings of the Foundation's science team to analyze projects and explain the impact those projects will have on the Everglades. Working with lots of different groups like politicians, planners, developers and the public, the science team tries to get agreement on working toward restoration of the Everglades. The fact that restoration is a good investment motivates a lot of people. Big surprise, huh?

Living in the Northeast, I almost never heard about the Everglades, but my Grandfather went there and told me all about it, including about how the Florida Panther is almost gone and about lots of serious problems having to do with water -- quality and quantity. Home to about 73 threatened or endangered species, the Everglades ecosystem faces overdevelopment that is taking over wild habitat. Heck, who could blame people for wanting to live in such a beautiful place and the area has such cool names, like Lake Okeechobee, Kissimmee and Palmetto Bay! Invasive exotic species (and I don't mean the folks coming down from up North) cause more problems. Burmese Pythons, originally brought in as pets, were released, loved the place and had babies. Since they don't have many enemies, they are trouble, as are the Australian Pines that are displacing the native plants. While the Everglades are sometimes thought of as a swamp they are really a slow moving river upon which eight million people rely for water. Earth to President Trump - Don't drain that swamp!

We took a family vacation to Florida and went snorkeling at John Pennekamp Coral Reef State Park (wow!) and also took an ecotour of the "River of Grass". So different from where I live. When I got back home I read an excellent ecomystery about a biology teacher, a tri-lingual macaw and some rompin' in the swamp, and started another book about a boat that is dumping disgusting raw sewage in the harbor and kids are trying to right the wrong. Guess what? The author is from Florida and was actually one of the speakers at your Everglades Foundation fundraiser, Mr. President!

P.S. He doesn't think kids are stupid and makes the characters real, like my snaggle-toothed Uncle Frank, who shows up sometimes for Thanksgiving dinner and tells the most hilarious stories, especially after he drinks out of his special secret little silver flat thermos that he keeps in his inside hidden jacket pocket. He has a lot of humorous expressions like "stinkier than a bag full of fresh farts". Mom doesn't think he is all that funny, but he is sure not a "fake" person, the way some kids' books make the characters.

Back in 1947, Marjory Stoneman Douglas coined that term for the Everglades in her book, "River of Grass", rejecting the commonly held belief that the Everglades was a swamp. She worked with scientists and called attention to the need for a conservation program to protect a valuable natural resource that many thought useful only if drained, dammed and developed.

Two kids have to figure out what is really going on when a biology teacher goes missing. I won't give you any spoilers. "Scat" by Carl Hiassen, 2012.

"Flush", Carl Hiaasen, 2010, reminded me of the water problems we have around here, where you can't go swimming some of the time because of raw sewage. Our dog sometimes drinks out of the

POLAR BEARS

First, I have to mention Polar Bears. I love to see Polar Bears in movies and on TV and I am worried about them. I have never seen a real one, except in the zoo, where it didn't look very happy or have a lot of room.

We learned there is a report card for the Arctic where a lot of Polar Bears live and this year it got failing marks because of global warming. 🦶

The Polar Bears need ice to live and climate change is making the ice melt.   🦶

In Science we learned there are 19 different kinds of Polar Bears. Some kinds aren't doing very well. We learned that by 2030 the Hudson Bay Polar Bear might all be gone because of global warming. 🦶

I will be 24 in 2030 and hope there are all kinds of Polar Bears left for me and other people to see in the wild.

🦶 Since 2006 The National Oceanic and Atmospheric Administration (NOAA) has issued an annual Arctic Report Card. One tidbit from the website, www.noaa.gov, is that the average surface air temperature for the year from 9/15 to 9/16 was the highest since 1900. That's 115 years! Lots of nitty gritty on that website.

🦶 Look at climate.nasa.gov the National Aeronautics and Space Administration (NASA) website for tons of info about climate change. At climatekids.nasa.gov go for a ride in the "Climate Time Machine" that lets you go back and forward in time to see how the Earth changes. Plus, there are directions for a bunch of crafts to make like "sun s'mores". Look here for science project ideas.

🦶 Some people don't believe in global warming at all, while some believe in global warming, but don't think human activity has any effect on it. They say what we the people do has no impact. They think it is OK to use a lot of fossil fuel, ignore the potential of alternative energy, and argue that the steps my family and I take are pretty much a waste of time. I say they are wrong, and so do lots of scientists, most in fact. Anyway, check out these "Climate Denier" sites to find out what they say: globalclimatescam.com Also, "Climate Change Skeptics Welcome Open Debate Under Trump Presidency", Thomas D. Williams, PhD., 1/2/17, www.breitbart.com. Also, there is a blog by Judith Curry, PhD, "Climate,etc." which has some info well beyond the basic level. https://judithcurry.com

THINGS WE DO TO HELP OUR PLANET

Some think that what we do doesn't make much of a difference, but it does and the more people who do things to help the environment, the bigger the difference will be. Jane Goodall, who went into the African jungle, studied and wrote about chimps, said, "You cannot get through a single day without having an impact on the world. What you do makes a difference and you have to decide what kind of difference you want to make." Knowing you can make a difference gives you power.

My family makes sure to turn off the lights when we are not using them and turn down the heat so we don't use too much fossil fuel, because using fossil fuel makes our planet warmer. A warmer planet means that the ice the Polar Bears need to live on melts and they have to struggle to survive.

Mr. President, you and the other people had it right when you said in your 2009 letter to President Obama that investing in a Clean Energy Economy will be good for business and help our planet.

Some people say you are a lot like Ronald Reagan, our 40th President, and my first name namesake. I read that he said, "Preservation of our environment is not a liberal or a conservative challenge, it's common sense." We are all in this together.

State of the Union Address 1/25/84

UNDER THE SEA

When I was 8, my family took a vacation and we went snorkeling in Florida. It was a little scary at first, but after awhile I forgot to be scared and it became beautiful. We swam with Parrot fish and other fish and sea turtles that were really, really huge and saw coral that was amazing colors.

Jack, the guy that took us out in his boat, warned us that we should enjoy it now because the coral reef is dying. That was sad. He said pollution, oil spills and climate change are killing the reefs and he will have to find a new job because nobody will want to see a zombie coral reef that is all bleached white with no fish. So, whatever you can do to save the reefs and fish and fight pollution, oil spills and climate change would be really, really good and would also help Jack keep working.

My brother, he's 14, says there is a very important agreement, the Paris Agreement, where all the countries promised they would help reduce pollution and slow down climate change. That sounds good to me, but I know you know a lot about making a good deal, "The Art of the Deal", so if you can make it even better for our planet, that would be great!

We all need to help and America can be exceptional, kind of like what you said in your important 2009 letter to President Obama, America can lead the way!

If you want to witness coral bleaching, check out news.nationalgeographic.com, a very scary time-lapse video.

One good place to check out the Paris Agreement is www.nature.com the website of the Nature Conservancy. 196 nations signed on, committing to take steps to prevent climate change and make the planet cleaner and safer for future generations - us and our kids. There is also some good info about the importance of funding the Land and Water Conservation Fund which protects our parks and other natural resources. The LWCF is playing a big part in trying to save the Florida Panther, of which there are only about 160 left.

20

THINGS WE DO TO HELP OUR PLANET

In our family we cut plastic netting and plastic six pack holders before we recycle them so they don't trap and kill the fish. We also bring reusable bags when we go grocery shopping so we don't need the plastic ones that blow all over and hang from trees. I read that by 2050, when I am 44, the pieces of plastic in the Oceans will weigh more than all the fish in the Oceans. I want to swim with fish, not plastic garbage!

We try to buy stuff that has less packaging and re-use newspaper for gift wrap, which looks prettier than it sounds. For a calendar I use what my Grandpa gave me - a metal calendar that you can use forever and don't have to throw away, a souvenir from his trip to Florida!

EARTH DAY 2017

FRESH WATER STREAMS AND LAKES

I know you want to make America great again. We live by one of the Great Lakes, Lake Erie, and my Grandfather (not my Great Grandfather LOL!) said it would be nice if you could make the Great Lakes great again, too. People used to fish and swim, but now a lot of the fish are gone or filled with toxins and you can't swim so much because there is sewage in the lake and signs that say "No Swimming" because of bacteria. How would you like it if the beautiful water by Mar-A-Lago stunk and you couldn't go in because it was so polluted and dead fish washed up all the time? Not so much, I bet.

We also need clean water to drink, so please do what you can to make sure our water is clean and gets tested like it should. Lately I've been hearing that you are going to cut funding by about 97% for the Great Lakes Restoration Initiative. Can that be true? I can't believe it. There must be some kind of mistake. PLEASE don't do that.

You said how it was really, really important to fix our infrastructures, which means buildings, roads and facilities. That sounds kind of boring, but I can tell you, that is really important and totally true. A lot of times the beach is closed because the sewage treatment plant and sewers are old and broken so the garbage goes right in the water. Yuck! Boy, sometimes it stinks pretty bad, like something my dog, Mr. Bigly, would roll around in. I think you are on the right track with fixing up the sewers.

We have a rain barrel to catch the rain and use it to water our garden. It helps prevent the runoff of storm water and other bad things that go into the lake making it so you can't swim. We don't waste water which is precious. Sometimes we make our own cleaning products because they are friendly to the environment. A simple formula is 1/2 cup of vinegar, 1/4 cup of baking soda mixed into 1/2 gallon of water. We use it to clean the tile floor in the kitchen and bathroom. It works, and it doesn't make Mr. Bigly sick if he licks the floor after we have cleaned it, which he does sometimes. Being a kid, I have to ask my folks or whoever is in charge if I can make it and use it.

EXTINCTION

At school we learned about extinct, which means totally all gone. Some animals have become extinct because of stuff we humans have done. My teacher told us about what happened to the passenger pigeon.

Once there were billions, really billions! They were hunted though, and up to 50,000 birds a day were killed. 🦶

The very last one lived in a zoo and was named Martha, after the First First Lady, Martha Washington. A singer with a guitar came to class and sang a beautiful but sad song about Martha. 🦶

I wish I had gotten a chance to see her. Now, Martha passed away and the passenger pigeons are extinct.

🦶 The Audubon website, www.audubon.org has a lot of good information about all kinds of birds and the environment. There I read an article about Martha called, "13 Memories of Martha, the Last Passenger Pigeon" by Chelsea Harvey and Elizabeth Newbern, 8/29/14.

🦶 "Martha, the Last of the Passenger Pigeons" is a song that was written and originally performed by John Herald. He used to be the lead singer and guitarist for a group called the Greenbriar Boys. You can hear it on Youtube and if you Google "John Herald" you will find out a lot about him.

Martha

LOSS OF HABITAT

Some animals in the wild, like the Bengal Tiger, the Giraffe and the Gorilla are in serious danger of becoming extinct, like Martha, so PLEASE don't let that happen. They are losing their habitat and being killed by poachers and hunters. Lots of animals that are endangered do not live in America, but there are still things you can do to help, like make sure to punish anybody from America that goes and illegally hunts an endangered animal. Maybe they could be charged a really, really "yuuuuge" fine that would go to support the animals' habitat and also discourage people from illegally hunting them.

Also, please make sure that people who smuggle endangered animal parts, like Bengal Tiger fur, ivory or rhinoceros horn, are punished so they don't do it. You can show the way!

All this makes me think what if our habitat was ruined and we were forced to choose between leaving our planet or becoming extinct. Where would we go? Colonize the Moon? Will we become refugees from Earth? What if there is no place else to go, or if no one wants to let us in? But, if we all do what we can to be good caretakers of Earth, including you and the people you appoint, I think we should be OK.

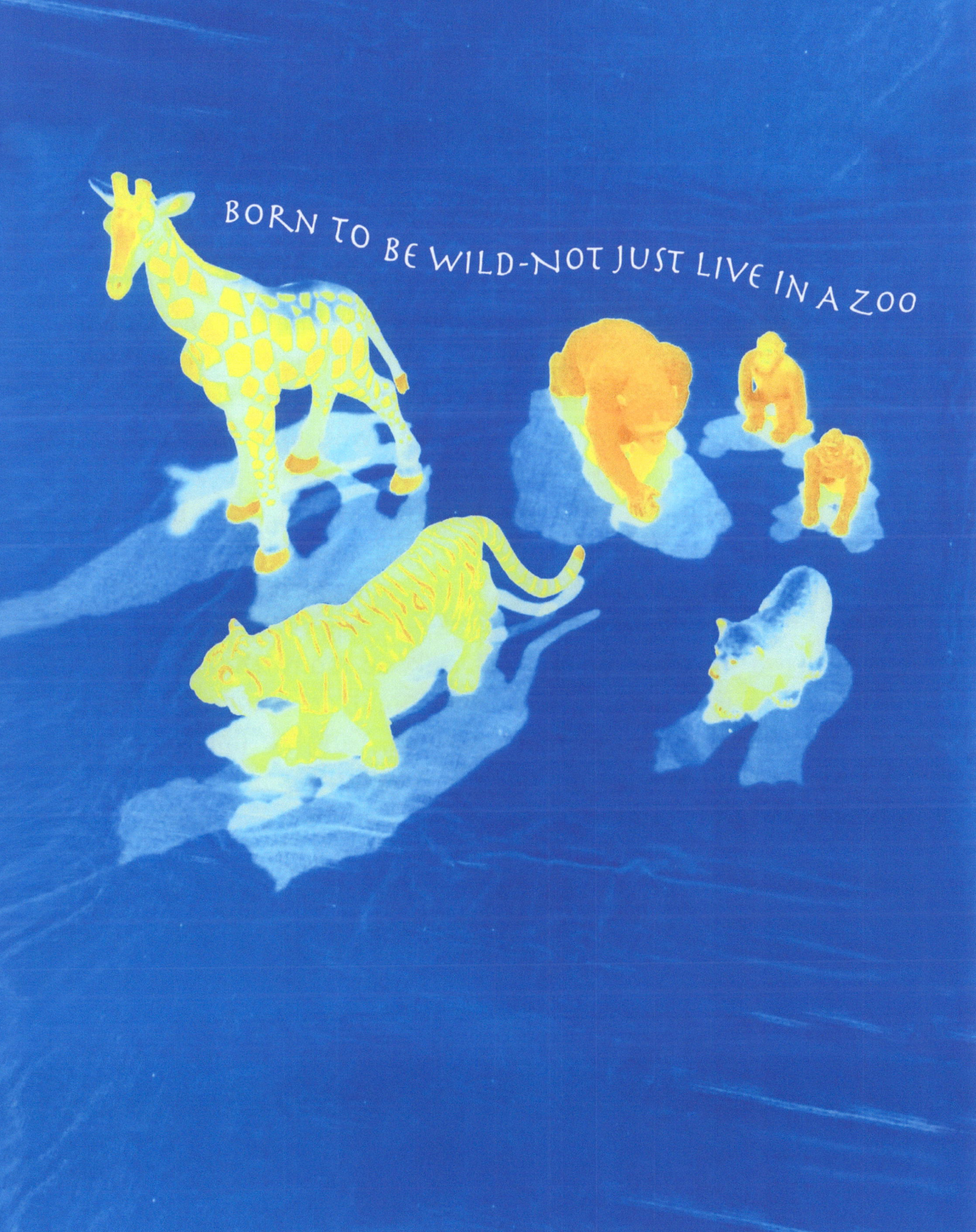

SOME ANIMALS THAT ARE PROBABLY EXTINCT-RECENT TIMES

The Golden Toad lived in Costa Rica and was really, really bright orange, like the color of a setting sun or a nylon pylon. In 1987 there was some crazy weather and of an estimated 30,000 toads only 29 survived. The last recorded sighting of the species, despite people searching, was 1 lone male in 1989. None since.

Also, the Baiji River Dolphin, called the "Goddess of the Yangtze", has been declared "functionally extinct". That means there are too few moms and dads around to make sure babies continue to be born. The Dolphins lived in the Yangtze River, and as China became industrialized, waste flowed into the river causing pollution that harmed them. More died when increased ship traffic caused collisions with the Dolphins which were blind. Finally, fishermen used nets that entangled the Dolphins. In the 1980's there were 400; in 1997, 13; in 2006 zero, none, nada.

There are a lot more animals at risk, so many that I ask "Imagine what if we didn't have any Sumatran elephants, black rhinos, Malayan tigers, mountain gorillas, Yangtze finless porpoises, or blue whales anymore?" Or any _____. You fill in the blank, Mr. President.

We always use recycled paper because that means less timber will be cut from the forests and it will help the animals keep their habitat. Some little creatures in the USA, like certain frogs, bumblebees and bugs are also in danger of becoming extinct. These little creatures might seem unimportant but they are not, because it is amazing how all the creatures really work together as part of a living miracle! For example, we need our bumblebees and honeybees because they pollinate our plants - no bees mean no tomatoes, watermelons, blueberries or lots of other fruits and veggies. That's almost like having no Summer!

> "If the bee disappeared off the surface of the globe, then man would have only 4 years of life left. No more bees, no more pollination, no more plants, no more animals, no more man."
> -Albert Einstein

There are both good and bad bugs. The good ones called beneficial insects help control the bad ones that would otherwise destroy our garden. Dragonflies eat gnats and mosquitoes. Lacewings eat mealybugs. Damsel bugs eat aphids and ground beetles eat the slugs that love to demolish our lettuce. So PLEASE don't let any animals become extinct because the balance of nature and biodiversity are really important. We don't even know how all the plants and animals fit together in nature, but if something goes extinct, it's like the song Martha says, "you know a piece of all of us goes with you".

When my Mom gardens she does not use poisons that would kill the bugs or birds. She has me pick off certain bugs from the plants. I throw them into a jar with soapy water that kills them. The kinds of bugs that are good for hand picking are Japanese Beetles (a nickel apiece) and red lily beetles (a dime apiece, and you'll see why). The red lily beetles are really something. They eat the stems, leaves, buds and flowers of the lilies. Demolition! The beetle is a scarlet red and has a really gross superpower – it makes a sticky, stinky brown disgusting poop (called a fecal shield) on the leaves, so you do not want to get anywhere near it! I wear gloves, hold my nose (it smells like when my baby brother puts up his fecal shield, LOL) and think about how the dimes are adding up, and my new skateboard is getting closer.

We also leave some of the garden a little wild so bugs and birds have a place to call home. Because our garden has a lot of seed heads and trees we get a lot of birds. Some kids and I take part in an annual bird count. 𝑓 We go outside and write down what birds we see. By being "citizen scientists" we track the bird population and can tell if it is growing or shrinking.

Our family also tries to eat more plants than animals because it is healthy, tastes great and is good for our planet.

I get to make dinner once in awhile and one of my favorite recipes is Buddha Bowl. You fill the bowl up round, like a Buddha's belly. There is no one recipe or right way to make it, and you can go with what you have and what people like. Generally it has veggies, grain, protein and some nuts or seeds. Here is one I make when the veggies come in from the garden. It requires some chopping and microwaving so make sure that you are OK to do that or get someone to help. All you do is arrange all the ingredients nicely in a bowl and put on a little of this dressing or any dressing you like.

𝑓 You can find out more about the annual Christmas bird count by Googling it or by looking on the Audubon website, www.audubon.org

BUDDHA BOWL RECIPE

lettuce leaves

carrots - use the peeler to make ribbons

cukes - just chop them

sweet peppers - cut into strips

chick peas –use canned and rinse and drain

tomatoes - cut up in slices or pieces

avocado - cut in strips

seeds - sunflower and sesame

package of quinoa and brown rice that comes in microwave bag
      (microwaved as per directions)

DRESSING

2 Tbsp vinegar, 1 tsp dijon mustard, 1 tsp. mayo, pinch of herb
(like thyme or tarragon), and/or chopped garlic, pinch of salt, a
little black pepper, 1/3 cup olive oil - mix or shake.

YOU NEED A GOOD TEAM, MR. PRESIDENT

I know you have an awful lot to do being President, and I know you can't do it alone, but you can choose some really, really good helpers. A good team can get an awful lot done. I was part of a science team in my 4th grade and our project about Anaerobic Digestion to Compost Food Waste won First Place in the All-County Fair. It sounds like a mouthful, which is funny because it's about food waste. Who knew we throw out up to 1/2 of our food that then rots and produces serious amounts of methane gas? There are ways to harness the energy that comes from the rotting food and some people are doing just that. The result? Food waste turns into a powerful environmental resource. The introduction of our paper is on the next page, check it out if you want to! We had a Science Advisor who gave us a lot of help. I hope you have a good Science Advisor.

You need a good team, too. I know you call the people who you pick a cabinet and it is not like a kitchen cabinet! I heard you say the cabinet you picked has the highest I.Q. of any cabinet ever. Wow, if you have the best and the brightest then things should turn out just fine, as long as your cabinet people are honest, work hard and are really knowledgeable about the environment. That would be really smart. Your cabinet helpers can report to you and to the people of our country about what is happening in the environment, so we know how it is going. Please have them do the reporting quickly though, because many scientists think that the climate is warming and pollution is happening faster than they first thought.

FOURTH GRADE SCIENCE FAIR FIRST PRIZE

Anaerobic Digestion to Repurpose Food Waste

Introduction

Food waste contributes to global warming by producing methane gas, which has a global warming potential that is far greater than carbon dioxide. It is estimated that up to one half of the food in the United States is thrown away, ending up in landfills where it decomposes, emitting methane gas. New York City alone generates about one million tons of organic waste every year.

Food waste also has the potential to positively impact our environment. It is a valuable source of fertilizer when composted - think about all the gardeners who save vegetable scraps for the compost pile, add leaves and grass clippings, wait for the earthworms to do their magic, and, voila, beautiful fertilizer for the garden. Unfortunately, on a commercial large scale level composting isn't always practical, especially in an urban environment. Space requirements and the fossil fuel swilling equipment required to process the compost mean the process isn't exactly environmentally friendly.

An alternative method of repurposing food waste, anaerobic digestion, yields both fertilizer and fuel, in an environmentally friendly way. An anaerobic digester is really just an airtight container, like a tank, filled with a special mixture of bacteria. The mixture is similar to what you would find in the stomach of a cow. As the food waste decomposes it produces solids, liquids and gases. The solids can be composted and made into fertilizers, as can the liquids. The gases produced, called biogas, can generate heat or electricity or can be processed into natural gas.

MAKE AMERICA GREAT

I am not sure if I was alive when things were really, really great and if I was, I was too little to remember. Now, while you are the President you have to do what it takes to make sure that our planet Earth is healthy and stays healthy for all living creatures or else America will not be great or even very good. Do it big league for our future.

That's all. Congratulations on winning. You did something almost no one thought you could do. Thank you for reading this long letter. My mom said I should make it into a book! Good Luck with making America great! I hope you get an A+ on your report cards for taking extra good care of our Country that we love.

It has taken me awhile to finish this letter, and I keep hearing things about your plans for the environment that make me more and more nervous. Aren't you the person who signed that letter to President Obama saying that we need meaningful and effective measures to prevent climate change? Then what the heck are you doing when you start rolling back the regulations that we need? I just don't get it. Maybe after you remember your letter and think about things you'll get back on track! I hope so.

I am not allowed to use Twitter yet, so please write back if you like, but don't Tweet me 'cause I won't see it. Stay green.

Your Friend,
Reagan Kennedy

SECOND LETTER

Dear President Trump,

I heard you answered a letter from a kid who wanted to mow the White House lawn, and also one from a kid who was a big fan. I felt a little sad because you have not answered my letter or letters from some other kids who wrote you about the environment. Certain things you have done since becoming President, like withdrawing from the Climate Treaty for just one example, made me disappointed. Also, and I don't mean to be disrespectful, but sometimes it seems like you say things without thinking them through and it makes the American people really divided and angry with each other. My Uncle Frank sometimes starts talking about stuff without thinking and my Grandma tells him to please shut his fool mouth before he gets us all angry and not talking to each other.   Anyway, I was feeling kind of down but I started hearing all kinds of things other people were doing about the environment to kind of pick up the slack. Over 350 mayors and 12 or more governors and over 300 plus big companies all committing to fighting climate change and carrying out the goals of the Climate Treaty. So, I am feeling hopeful and will not give up but will double down on what my friends and I can do. Check out our website, www.reagankennedy.org   And don't think I have completely given up on you - you are still President, which is to say kind of a big deal, and maybe you can be made to see what is going on and do something positive- that is our hope.   Look forward to hearing from you, but not holding my breath.

Sincerely,

Reagan Kennedy

For Educators, Parents and Readers- Discussion Points

1. Proponents of legal big game hunting -- "trophy hunting" in Africa point out that the mega dollars which these safaris bring in is used to support conservation efforts and also provide local people with jobs guarding the animals from poachers. Opponents say that killing the beautiful wild animals for sport can never be justified, and also argue that not all that much money is really channeled to animal welfare. What do you think? Can there ever be a "good balance" that allows the hunting of certain endangered animals to provide for the protection of other endangered animals? What about the role of creating jobs for local people? What if the animals were used for food?

2. Some people accept climate change as a fact but deny that human behavior has a role. What do you think? Does what we do individually on a daily basis matter in such a large world?

3. Should scientists bring back extinct species? Some scientists think that dedicating research funds and time to "de-extincting" certain long gone species is worthwhile and even a moral obligation, while others see potential danger in that we would again be altering the "natural" biodiversity. Who is right?

4. People who are most exposed to polluted environments are often the poor and people of color. Why would poor communities be used for things like toxic dumps, landfills, and industrial plants? How does the idea of environmental justice fit in with other environmentalism?

****

Check out our website, www.reagankennedy.org for additional ideas, information, activities and a lot of excitement about kid powered environmentalism. You can even post your own letter to the President.

Epilogue

Even though I'm named after two presidents, I'm not really into politics. You've got your Democrats, Republicans, Conservatives, Liberals, Libertarians, Socialists, Conservatarians and probably a lot more. That's about all I know about that. What I am into is nature and science and looking stuff up. Investigating. Cool info is to be had at your fingertips. How about this - the Fang Blenny is a fish that has two humungous teeth and some can shoot venom containing opioid like substances that send any predator into a drugged out disoriented daze while the little Blenny escapes! So I look up stuff and listen to some science podcasts and that's how I got a lot of information for my letter to President Trump, being careful to check my sources for accuracy.

Late November had everybody buzzing about the election. Some people were thrilled and some horrified. Both anticipating extreme change. The horrified feared that when Donald Trump became President he would sign a death sentence for the environment. Bye bye water and air quality. Climate change deniers would rule. Endangered wildlife - gone. Science kicked to the curb. I thought no. I hoped no. Maybe if I wrote and lots of others, especially kids, wrote and told the President about how we need to take care of our planet, let him know we are watching, he'd get on the right track.

I started my letter in December, 2016. I had hope because in 2009 in the days before the Copenhagen Convention on climate change he signed a letter published in the New York Times, (a copy is in the book) urging President Obama to support the Clean Energy Economy, reduce harmful emissions and saying the United States should model the change necessary to protect our planet from the destruction of climate change. Way to go!

Now it's late March and I'm not so hopeful. The President named a guy to head the EPA (Environmental Protection Agency, they are in charge of the rules) who doesn't seem to think much of the EPA and who is a climate change skeptic.

Also, in looking stuff up, I see President Trump had this advisor, Myron Edell, who said, "The green movement is the greatest threat to freedom." So me, recycling bottles, I'm a threat to freedom? Now that's scary.

Great Lakes funding decimated or eliminated? And what should we call the Great Barrier Reef if climate change continues unabated? Instead of the United States leading the way in cleaning up the planet, as President Trump urged in 2009, will it be China?

If I don't stop writing, I won't be able to get this published and out to you, so I'm stopping. Please write your letter, urging the President to be a responsible steward of our future. Thanks. Stay green (even if some people think it's scary). R.K.

About the Author -
Meet Reagan Kennedy a/k/a

Lisa McDougall

Version one has Reagan Kennedy as a precocious but naive environmental scientist wannabe. A ten year old who simply believes there is a good chance that Trump will do right by the environment. Seriously? On what possible basis? Reagan's older brother shared a copy of a December 6, 2009 letter that ran as a full page ad in the New York Times. Guess what? Trump and others wrote to Obama acknowledging the scientific basis for climate change and urging action lest there be consequences both imminent and irreversible. The message is clear, loud and strong. Hat hanger number one for Reagan, apparently unaware that Trump can blow hot and cold. And hat hanger two, as per Reagan's logic -Trump has a personal stake in the future of a healthy planet - look at his loving family, including children and grandchildren. The final convincer for Reagan is that Trump is self proclaimed as smart, very, very smart, even a genius, so Reagan believes duh, of course Trump gets it. Reagan reflects the wonder and awe that a child sees in nature and questions how anyone with power could not use that power for life affirming purposes, taking literally the words that come out of people's mouths because words matter.

Version two, maybe Reagan is at heart a Bernie Sanders supporter intent on exposing hypocrisy and the impending ruin of the environment by Trump appointees who possess a slash and burn, take no prisoners mentality, reporting to a president who is complicit, ignorant or doesn't care, or all of the above. The same President who says he is an environmentalist. The passion of Sanders' supporters inspire Reagan to write a letter to the President. Reagan shows some friends. They like it. Say they will also write to the President so he knows they are watching, concerned. Reagan then makes the letter into this book. More kids read it. A kids' movement. Lots and lots of kids writing letters to the President. Kids learning more about science to be ready to recognize falsehoods. Kids becoming citizen scientists. Kids educating their families on going green and staying green. Kids visualizing their future. Kids calling out any hypocrisy or environmental degradation. Kids mobilizing parents. Kids organizing. They get it. You get it.

Truth be told, as it should be, Reagan Kennedy is in a sense both versions. Reagan is the child within Lisa McDougall, who is the adult who transcribed and illustrated Reagan Kennedy's hopes, thoughts and feelings.